Does the
YETI
Exist?

Nick Hunter

Raintree is an imprint of Capstone Global Library Limited, a company incorporated in England and Wales having its registered office at 264 Banbury Road, Oxford, OX2 7DY – Registered company number: 6695582

www.raintree.co.uk
myorders@raintree.co.uk

Edited by Helen Cox Cannons
Designed by Steve Mead
Original illustrations © Capstone Global Library Ltd 2016
Picture research by Kelly Garvin
Production by Victoria Fitzgerald
Originated by Capstone Global Library Ltd
Printed and bound in China

ISBN 978 1 4747 1474 7 (hardback)
19 18 17 16 15
10 9 8 7 6 5 4 3 2 1

ISBN 978 1 4747 1492 1 (paperback)
20 19 18 17 16
10 9 8 7 6 5 4 3 2 1

British Library Cataloguing in Publication Data
A full catalogue record for this book is available from the British Library.

Acknowledgements
Alamy: Daily Mail/Rex, 11 (bottom), 21, (b), Steven Finn, 19 (top), The Natural History Museum, 32 (b); Fortean Picture Library, 9 (top right), 27 (bottom right), 40 (left); Corbis: Bettmann, 16 (middle), Christian Kober, 22 (b), 23; Getty Images: Christof Stache/ullstein bild, 20 (b), Dave Buresh/The Denver Post, 26 (br), Ernst Haas, 17 (b), Express Newspapers/Hulton Archive, 14 (bottom left), Keystone/Hulton Archive, 24 (b), Hulton Archive/Topical Press Agency, 15 (top left), The Image Bank, 8 (b); iStockphoto, cover; Minden Pictures: Mark Newman, 30 (b), Tui De Roy, 25 (b); National Geographic Creative, 13 (b); Science Source: Christian Jegou Publiphoto Diffusion, 31 (b); Shutterstock: Agrus, 41 (t), AlexsandrN, 28-29 (top background), andreiuc88, cover, Avatar_023, 14-15 (background), BigganVi 6-7 (background), Bobb Klissourski, 18 (tl), Calin Tatu, 5 (m), Chayatorn Laorattanavech, 24-25 (background), Christian Mueller, 20-21 (background), Csehak Szabolcs, 12-13 (background), Dennis W. Donohue, 33 (b), Esteban De Armas, 30 (background), forbis, 7 (m), gbreezy, 33 (tr), GROGL 22, icedmocha, 24 (tr), Intrepix, 11 (middle right), Ivan Baranov, 8 (tl), Izf, 29 (tr), javarman, 41 (background), Kozoriz Yuriy, 32-33 (background), Kunal Mehta, 8-9 (background), LAND, 16-17 (background), Leigh Prather, 25 (b), Lightspring, 26-27 (background), meunierd, 28-29 (bottom background), Nik Merkulov, 40, oksmit, 36 (l), Olga Danylenko, 6 (b), outdoorsman, 34 (l), Paisan Changhirun, 31, (background), Reno Martin, 10-11 (background), R.M. Nunes, 38-39, Sergey Nivens, 34-35 (background), Vadim Petrakov, 12 (b), 41 (b), Vesna Longton, 36-27 (background); The Image Works: Fortean/TopFoto, 18 (b); Wikimedia/Wanida W., 28 (b)
Artistic elements: Shutterstock: agsandrew, Bruce Rolff, Eky Studio, Maksim Kabakou, Nik Merkulov

CONTENTS

MISSION ABOMINABLE!

Welcome! I'm glad you could come. I'm the Mystery Master. I'm here to solve mysteries and explore the unexplained. I've been looking for someone like you for a while.

How would you like to explore one of the world's great wildernesses? You'll be trying to find answers high up in the Himalaya Mountains of Asia. Since ancient times we've been getting reports of a mysterious creature in this region. Local people are sure the creature exists and mountaineers claim to have seen evidence of a huge hairy beast that walks on two legs. It has been called the Abominable Snowman, but to locals it is the Yeti.

Your mission is to use all the available evidence to try to solve this puzzle once and for all:

DOES THE YETI EXIST?

Mount Annapurna, Himalayas, 1970

British climber Don Whillans was on an expedition to climb Annapurna at an altitude of 3,962 metres (13,000 feet) when he saw footprints in the snow. They were too big to be made by any human.

Later, Whillans looked out of his tent and saw an ape-like creature moving across the snow on four legs. The climber also heard strange animal cries in the distance. His Sherpa guide believed the cries were of a Yeti. Whillans said, "It bounded out of the shadows and headed straight up the slope in the absolutely bright moonlight. It looked like an ape. I don't think it was a bear."

If the Yeti is real, it's living high up in these mountains.

INVESTIGATION TIPS

WARNING!
Remember, not all the evidence you'll find is reliable. Keep on the lookout for made-up or mistaken eyewitness accounts, fake photos and some ideas that are just plain crazy. Your job is to find the truth.

How to be a Yeti investigator

If you want to uncover the secrets of the Yeti, you'll have to analyse all the evidence very carefully. Many explorers and local people have discovered mysterious footprints in the snow. Some even claim to have seen the Yeti. You need to separate legends and stories from hard scientific evidence.

Solving problems

Your most powerful tool in the hunt for the Yeti is your brain. Use it to work out which evidence you can trust and test different theories about the Yeti. Scientists can use the very latest techniques to analyse a single hair and tell you if it belongs to an animal we already know about or whether it's something new and undiscovered.

The people of the Himalayas know the mountains and stories about the Yeti better than anyone.

If you venture into the mountains, you need to be prepared for extreme cold and danger – one false move could mean falling to your death. You may even have to defend yourself against an angry Yeti!

Yeti discovery kit

If you want to go in search of the Yeti, make sure you pack some essential equipment:

- Warm clothing: The high passes of the Himalayas are one of the most extreme places on Earth. Any exposed skin could suffer frostbite in the freezing mountains.

- Mountaineering gear: You'll need ropes, ice axes and even breathing equipment to stay alive in the thin air of the Himalayas.

- Camera: You'll want to photograph all the evidence, especially if you see any mysterious creatures in the distance or footprints in the snow.

- Global Positioning System (GPS), map and compass: Get lost in the Himalayas and you may not live long enough to find the Yeti.

TOP SECRET

Sometimes the best evidence is not always what you want to carry around with you. An American expedition collected samples of what they thought was Yeti poo.

THE EVIDENCE:
The story begins

The people of Nepal and other countries of the Himalayas have told stories about the Yeti for hundreds of years. Its name comes from the Sherpa language: from *yeh-teh*, meaning "animal of rocky places" or *meh-teh* meaning "man-bear". More than 2,300 years ago, Alexander the Great, born in Macedonia, southern Europe, led an army into what is now India. He had heard stories of the Yeti and demanded to see one, but the people he met said that the Yeti would not survive outside the high mountains.

The Himalayas cover a huge area and local cultures do not all share the same beliefs about the Yeti. For some it is a strange and magical beast; for others it is just another animal, which occasionally attacks livestock and people.

Alexander the Great was one of the first people to be intrigued by the Yeti legend.

A mountain mystery

In the 20th century, mountaineers from around the world began to visit the Himalayas. They heard the stories and the visitors began to report sightings of a creature taller than a person, standing up on two legs. Was it possible that a previously unknown creature had stayed hidden in the remote wilderness of the world's highest mountain range?

Descriptions of the Yeti vary, but most include these features:
- Ape-like creature around 2 metres (6.5 feet) tall
- Stands on two legs
- Covered in grey or brown hair
- Powerful, muscular build

TOP SECRET

In the 1950s, the government of Nepal sold licences to expeditions searching for the Yeti. The US government produced some rules for Yeti hunters:

- They had to buy a permit from the Nepalese government.

- Explorers could take photos of a Yeti or capture it alive, but they could not kill or shoot at a Yeti unless they were attacked.

- Anyone who found a Yeti would have to show their evidence to Nepal's government before making their amazing discovery public.

MEETINGS WITH YETIS

Many people claim to have seen Yetis. Have a look at these stories. Do you think they are genuine?

EYEWITNESS

Villagers in India, 2007

Villagers in north-eastern India, on the edge of the Himalayas, were terrified by several sightings of "hairy giants" in the area. One farmer claimed to have seen a whole family of the creature, which was called Jungle Man. Government investigators could not find conclusive proof of what the villagers had seen.

INVESTIGATION TIPS

Eyewitness accounts
How do you know these witnesses are telling the truth? An eyewitness account is more convincing if more than one person saw the same thing. Ask yourself if the eyewitness has any reason to make the story up. If they already believed in the Yeti, maybe they did not consider other ways of explaining what they saw.

Many people saw these beasts. Were they Yetis or some other type of known animal such as an ape?

Tombazi thought the figure he saw was human, but the footprints were too small.

Photographer N.A. Tombazi was part of a Royal Geographical Society expedition exploring at about 4,572 metres (15,000 feet) above sea level when he saw a creature more than 200 metres (656 feet) away:
"Unquestionably the figure in outline was exactly like a human being, walking upright and stopping occasionally to pull at some dwarf rhododendron bushes. It showed up dark against the snow and, as far as I could make out, wore no clothes."

Tombazi did not have time to take a photo, but he examined the footprints left by the possible Yeti, which were shorter and wider than human footprints.

HIMALAYAS

INDIA

As more climbers travelled to the Himalayas, the number of Yeti sightings increased.

WHEN YETIS ATTACK

Witnesses who claim to have seen Yetis often only catch a glimpse of a distant figure, or other signs such as footprints. Tibetan yak-herder Lhakpa Dorma suffered a terrifying ordeal in 1974, in which she may have survived a close encounter with a Yeti.

Dorma was tending her herd in a remote Himalayan valley when the incident happened. She was found unconscious and surrounded by the bodies of yaks. When she recovered, the young woman was convinced that the scene of devastation was caused by a Yeti, which had grabbed her from behind before ferociously attacking the yaks.

THE SCIENCE

Finding food

All animals have to eat. If a Yeti really attacked Lhakpa Dorma's yaks, we can deduce that Yetis are carnivores, or meat-eaters. Dorma said the Yeti she saw had large teeth. Yetis would have to venture down below the snow-line to find food, so why aren't there more stories of Yeti attacks on people and animals?

Reasonable doubts?

Lhakpa Dorma really believed a Yeti attacked her. She described it in detail, but could she have made a mistake? There are other predators, such as bears, living in the region. Dorma was also unconscious when she was discovered. How would you go about checking the details of her story?

This incredible story has been retold many times and some of the details are unclear. The Yeti described by Dorma was supposedly just 1.2 metres (4 feet) tall, smaller than other reported sightings.

What other creatures could have attacked Lhakpa Dorma and her animals?

FOOTPRINTS IN THE SNOW

In the 1950s, mountaineers flocked to the Himalayas, to climb the perilous peaks but also to search for the Yeti. In 1951, Eric Shipton was leading a team of climbers across a deserted glacier close to Mount Everest, the world's highest peak, when they discovered a trail of footprints heading down the glacier.

The prints were about 30 centimetres (12 inches) long and 15 centimetres (6 inches) wide, much wider than a human foot. Anyway, the climbers knew that they were the only people in the area. If the prints were not human, what were they?

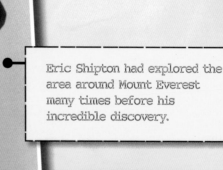

Eric Shipton had explored the area around Mount Everest many times before his incredible discovery.

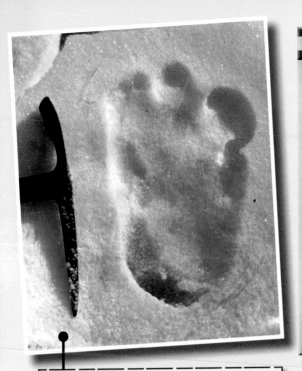

Not everyone believes Shipton's story of the Yeti footprint. Expedition doctor, Michael Ward, later revealed that the famous photo was just one of many tracks they saw, which were not all the same. Other expedition members claimed that Shipton liked practical jokes and making up stories. Was the footprint one of those jokes?

Does this photograph really show the footprint of a Yeti?

Photographic evidence

Luckily, Shipton and his team took photographs of the footprints. The shape of some had been distorted by melting snow around the edges, but others were very clear. The experienced climbers believed these prints had been made by something they had not encountered before, and the photos caused a rush to the Himalayas to find out more.

INVESTIGATION TIPS

Footprint questions

Although we have pictures of the footprints, with an ice axe to show the size, we may not know the full story. Footprints in snow can change shape as the sun melts the snow around its edges.

EDMUND HILLARY'S YETI HUNT

Edmund Hillary was part of Shipton's expedition, although he was exploring elsewhere when the footprints were found. In 1953, Hillary and Tenzing Norgay shot to global fame when they became the first climbers to reach the summit of Mount Everest. After this great feat, Hillary was determined to uncover the secrets of the Yeti.

Edmund Hillary (right) and Tenzing Norgay did not discover any signs of a Yeti during their climb of Mount Everest.

TOP SECRET

Tenzing Norgay wrote that he believed in the Yeti because his father had seen one. However, he became less sure about the existence of the creature later in life.

In 1960, Hillary set off to find answers in the Himalayas. His team included several scientists as well as experienced climbers. At a Buddhist monastery deep in the mountains, they were shown a precious and ancient piece of animal hide. Could it be, as the monks claimed, the ancient scalp of a Yeti?

Forensic tests were used to separate fact from legend. The relic was tested in London, Paris and Chicago. It was certainly rare and ancient, but the shocking truth was that it had never been part of a Yeti.

The Yeti legend

As the scientific tests failed to find evidence of Yetis, Hillary became convinced that the Yeti was legend and not a real creature at all. He recognized that the Sherpa people of the mountains believed in the Yeti as a magical creature rather than a real animal: "To a Sherpa the ability of a Yeti to make himself invisible at will is just as important a part of description as his probable shape and size." In spite of Edmund Hillary's doubts, the search continued.

TOP SECRET

The "Yeti scalp" (shown here) was probably made from the skin of a serow, a type of Himalayan goat. Yeti skins that the team collected were proven to have come from a brown bear.

THE LOST HAND OF A YETI

In 2008, researchers at the Royal College of Surgeons in London discovered something very unusual hidden in its huge collection: a box labelled "Yeti's finger". Inside the box was a finger about 9 centimetres (3½ inches) long and 2 centimetres (¾ inch) wide with a long nail. Had it once been attached to a hairy Himalayan hand? The story of how it got to London is one of the strangest in the whole mystery.

The finger had come from the Pangboche monastery in Nepal, where it had been part of a supposed Yeti's hand. Yeti explorer Peter Byrne managed to take one finger of the hand during an expedition in 1959, replacing it with a human finger.

The finger then went on a bizarre and secret journey. It was smuggled out of Nepal with the help of film star James Stewart, who was travelling in the area. Eventually the finger arrived in Britain, where it was tested by scientist William Charles Osman Hill. Osman Hill later donated it to the museum.

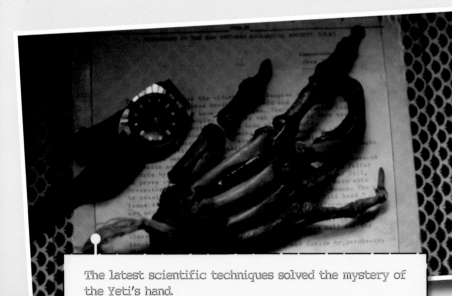

The latest scientific techniques solved the mystery of the Yeti's hand.

Slick expeditions

The "Yeti's finger" was the main piece of evidence discovered during the expeditions funded by American millionaire Tom Slick in the late 1950s. Slick and his team also collected samples of fur and dung that they hoped would come from some unknown beast, but everything they found could be linked to previously known animals.

TOP SECRET

The "Yeti's finger" was possibly the most unusual thing in the Royal College of Surgeons' collection, but only just. It also contains Winston Churchill's false teeth and half of mathematician Charles Babbage's brain.

THE SCIENCE

The truth

When he examined the finger, Osman Hill concluded that it belonged to a relative of modern humans. In 2011, using the latest scientific techniques, researchers confirmed that the finger was human after all.

EXPEDITIONS INTO THE UNKNOWN

You've probably worked out by now that plenty of people have tried to solve this mystery before you, including Tom Slick, Edmund Hillary and many others. During the 1960s, the Chinese, Russians and Americans competed against each other to be the first to find evidence of the Yeti. In 1986, one of the world's leading climbers set out to find the truth.

Reinhold Messner

Reinhold Messner was one of the greatest climbers in history. He scaled Everest without the help of breathing equipment in 1978 and went on to climb all the world's highest peaks. When Messner encountered a problem, he usually overcame it. In 1986, Messner was certain he had seen and heard a Yeti, walking on two legs. He vowed to solve the mystery.

Reinhold Messner is one of the world's greatest climbers, having climbed the 14 highest peaks on Earth.

Messner explored all the evidence he could find:

- In the secretive mountain kingdom of Bhutan, he was shown the supposed remains of a Yeti cub, which turned out to be fake.

- He went with local people to explore lairs of the Yeti, but they were in fact caves used by bears.

- He heard many stories of how Yetis had killed yaks and people.

Messner never found the proof he was looking for. In the end, he decided that the Yetis of the local myths and stories were actually bears.

In spite of Messner's conclusion, the search continues. In 2008, a Japanese expedition discovered what they believed were more Yeti footprints.

In 1954, the British *Daily Mail* newspaper sent a major expedition to the Himalayas including explorers, scientists and more than 300 porters to carry their equipment.

HUNTING FOR THE YETI

Perhaps the only way to find the truth would be to trek into the mountains to search for the Yeti yourself. If you do, beware as weather conditions can change in an instant. Exploring at high altitude can also lead to people seeing things that aren't really there, due to the effects of breathing thinner air at high altitudes.

THE SCIENCE

Going to extremes

We all need to breathe oxygen to live and it's in short supply in the mountains. Each breath you take of thinner mountain air contains less oxygen than air at lower levels. Almost all climbers in the region use breathing equipment. Lack of oxygen means climbers get tired quickly and can also affect brain function, so they can see and hear things that aren't there. This could explain some Yeti sightings.

Explorers in the Himalayas need to be prepared for extreme conditions and must use breathing equipment like this.

Stone-cold certain

Scientist Anthony Wooldridge was crossing the Himalayas on a long-distance run in 1986, when a dark figure on the horizon stopped him in his tracks. "The head was large and squarish and the whole body appeared to be covered with dark hair, although the upper arm was a slightly lighter colour."

Wooldridge was a long way from the creature, but the photos he took were closely examined by Yeti enthusiasts and seemed to be genuine. It was only later when Wooldridge returned to the same area that he realized the motionless Yeti was still in exactly the same place. It was actually a rock.

Danger zone

Dangers to look out for while mountain climbing include:

- *Avalanches*: These deadly floods of snow can travel down a mountainside at up to 130 kilometres (80 miles) per hour. If an avalanche starts above you, try to shelter behind a rock overhang, lie flat and try to keep your head above the deepening snow.

- *Crevasses*: When crossing a glacier, beware of these deep cracks in the ice. They can be hidden by snow. Fall in one and you may never get out. It's difficult enough to survive in the Himalayas, without keeping an eye out for Yetis in the distance.

Mysterious creatures

The Yeti is not the only creature out there that is rumoured to exist but not yet proven. The study of these mysterious creatures is called cryptozoology and the legendary animals themselves are called cryptids. If one of these creatures could be discovered, it would help to persuade people that the Yeti is still out there somewhere.

The Loch Ness Monster, Scotland

Nessie is one of the most famous of these mysterious creatures. The Loch Ness Monster could be a plesiosaur, a sea creature left over from the age of the dinosaurs. In spite of several supposed sightings, photos and scientific surveys, the lake has failed to reveal any secrets.

This photo of the Loch Ness Monster was later proved to be a hoax. It was created using some plastic and a toy submarine.

Mokele Mbembe, Congo basin, Africa

Deep in the Congo basin of Africa, explorers have searched for many years for the last of the dinosaurs. Many local people claim to have seen Mokele Mbembe, describing it as a long-necked dinosaur the size of an elephant, but no conclusive scientific evidence that it exists has ever been found.

Almasti, central Asia

The people of mountainous central Asia, to the northwest of the Himalayas, have many legends about the "wild man of the snows". Unlike the Yeti, the Almasti is similar to a human rather than an ape, but is covered in hair.

The most similar cryptid to the Yeti is believed by some to roam the forests of North America. Its name is Bigfoot or Sasquatch.

THE SCIENCE

Nature's secrets

There are probably species of living things still to be discovered. Many of these are likely to be minibeasts, but scientists recently discovered the first carnivorous mammal to be identified in the Americas in 35 years. The olinguito is a kind of raccoon. It was discovered by analysing bones stored in a Chicago museum, but living examples were later found in the forests of South America.

THE SECRETS OF BIGFOOT

The forests of North America are a long way from the Himalayas, but those who have seen Bigfoot, or the Sasquatch, describe it in similar ways to the Yeti. Witnesses talk of a large hairy ape, walking on two legs and, this won't come as a surprise, big five-toed feet. Why does it matter? Well, if there is a mysterious unknown ape in North America, why shouldn't there be one in the Himalayas?

Native Americans had told legends of Bigfoot for centuries, but the modern fascination with this creature rests on the eyewitness account of William Roe. Roe gave a detailed description of an ape-like creature he had seen while hiking in 1955. Unfortunately, Roe was on his own, so no one else could back up his description.

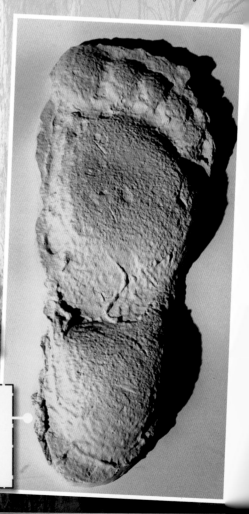

William Roe waited two years before telling anyone about his meeting with Bigfoot. Would you be able to keep a secret like that?

Sasquatch investigators in North America have taken many plaster casts of giant footprints.

Bigfoot on film

Roe's was the first of many reports of Bigfoot. In 1967, Roger Patterson and Bob Gimlin set out to end the mystery once and for all by filming Bigfoot. Amazingly, they returned with a film that showed a creature just like the one Roe had described. Does this mean the mystery of Bigfoot is solved? Some people are convinced, but others claim the animal in the film is a man in a gorilla suit.

INVESTIGATION TIPS

The Bigfoot film: history or hoax?

After many decades, no one has been able to prove that Patterson and Gimlin's film is real. If it is so easy to find and film Bigfoot, why has no one else managed to do it? Today, many of us have video cameras on our smartphones, but there have been no more Bigfoot films. Many people who knew Patterson have also raised questions about his character, saying he was well capable of planning a hoax.

Patterson took his Bigfoot film on tour. Even if it was a hoax, the film was very successful.

FURRY FAKES AND HIMALAYAN HOAXES

As an investigator, you need to be constantly on your guard to spot fakes and hoaxes. You may wonder why people would bother pretending to find evidence of the Yeti or other cryptids. The answer is usually money or fame.

The Snow Walker

In 1996, a TV channel broadcast a film called *The Snow Walker* that supposedly showed footage of a real Yeti. It promised to solve the mystery and reveal the secrets of the Yeti. It later emerged that the film had been created by the TV programme's producers. It fooled people just long enough to attract viewers to watch the TV channel.

Some fakes are more obvious than others!

Capturing a Yeti

In 2011, stories emerged from the Russian region of Ingushetia that a creature like Bigfoot or Yeti had been captured alive. The story spread fast on the internet but the authorities soon confirmed that the captured creature was actually a man in a suit. It seems that the stunt was staged to attract visitors to a new national park.

Digital cameras and smartphones mean it is easier than ever to take pictures of creatures - but also to edit them.

INVESTIGATION TIPS

Spotting a fake

It's not always easy to tell if something's a hoax. Computers and digital cameras make it easy for people to alter films and photos to show amazing things such as a real Yeti. Here are some tips to help you spot fakes:

- Don't just look at the video or photo, find out the story around it. If someone claims to have seen a Yeti, were they actually in the place they claim to have seen it?

- Just as with any eyewitness report, ask whether there were any other witnesses?

- Look closely at the film to see if there's anything that doesn't look right.

- Think about the witness. Has he or she been searching for evidence for years or was this first time lucky?

What else could the Yeti be?

In 1948, three army officers trekking in the Himalayas at a height of around 3,962 kilometres (13,000 feet) above sea level saw two large animals running towards them on two legs. Were they about to come face to face with the Yeti? In the end, the animals turned out to be langur monkeys, which can walk on two legs for long distances. What other animals in the Himalayas could be confused with the Yeti?

Two of the most likely candidates are:
* *Tibetan blue bear.* This very rare bear is actually grey or black.
* *Brown bear.* Large bear that can rear up on its hind legs. It lives on plants and animals such as goats and sheep.

Bears are large animals that can survive in the cold of the Himalayas. Many of the supposed Yeti footprints could have been made by bears.

The Tibetan blue bear is one of the rarest subspecies of bear.

Human relatives?

One theory is that the Yeti could be closely related to humans. Neanderthals were close prehistoric relatives of modern humans, living across much of Europe and Asia until around 35,000 years ago. Their stocky bodies were adapted to living in cold environments. A few thousand years after modern humans arrived in Europe from Africa, fossil evidence tells us that the Neanderthals died out. Some cryptozoologists think they could have survived in remote regions like the Himalayas. They believe it is possible that those early humans became wild and the legend of the Yeti was born.

It's a nice idea but, as yet, no physical evidence has been found to support it. Neanderthals were humans who used tools and even wore clothes. Could they have lost all these skills?

APE ANCESTORS

In 1935, German geologist Gustav von Koenigswald discovered a large fossilized tooth at a Chinese market. The tooth came from a giant ape, an ancient ancestor of the orangutan, which Koenigswald called Gigantopithecus. Although only a few remains of these great apes have been found, experts estimate they were about 3 metres (10 feet) tall. This would make it much bigger than the gorilla. It may have looked something like descriptions of the Yeti.

TOP SECRET

All scientific evidence points to the Gigantopithecus having died out many thousands of years ago. However, people have claimed to have had close encounters with huge apes in Southeast Asia since then. Are there more secrets to be revealed about this hairy enigma?

Our knowledge of Gigantopithecus is based on a few fossils such as its jawbone (above, right), shown next to a human one.

Ancestor of the Yeti?

Is it possible that Gigantopithecus could be the distant ancestor of the Yeti? Some experts certainly think so. But there are also a few problems with this theory:

- Although no full skeleton of this great ape has been found, it almost certainly did not have the human-like feet that created the famous Yeti footprints.
- Gigantopithecus probably died out about 200,000 years ago. If its descendants had survived, scientists would expect to find more than the few fossilized teeth and jaws that have emerged up to now.

THE SCIENCE

Hiding out

Do you find it hard to believe that the Yeti could stay hidden despite all attempts to find it? Other animals have been able to remain hidden for long periods. Scientists only discovered the mountain gorilla in 1902. Today there are around 800 of them living in the highlands of central Africa. If Yetis exist, there are probably very few of them.

DNA
Breakthrough

Just when it seemed that Yeti hunters were running out of ideas in their quest to solve this mystery, a scientist at the University of Oxford, thousands of kilometres from the snowy peaks of the Himalayas, made a remarkable discovery.

Professor Bryan Sykes collected hair samples from around the world that could have belonged to unknown animals. He tested the DNA of the samples. DNA is the material in every living cell that gives each living thing its unique features. Most of the samples were easily identifiable, but the researchers got very excited over two particular samples.

One sample came from an animal shot by a hunter in northern India and the other from some animal fur found in Bhutan, close to the Nepalese heartland of the Yeti legend. The DNA in both samples matched that of an ancient polar bear that existed more than 40,000 years ago. The discovery suggests that the Yeti could be an unidentified species of bear.

Polar bears do not live in the Himalayas, but some people believe they could be a distant relative of the Yeti.

The work of Sykes and his team does not help those who believe the Yeti is a huge ape, but it does mean that there could be something new out there to be discovered.

How does DNA testing work?

Every cell in an animal's body from its hair to its toenails contains a complete set of its DNA sequence. Animals of the same species share almost all the same DNA. By testing cells from an animal, scientists can tell if it is a member of a known species, such as a bear. If the DNA sequence is sufficiently different from other known species of animal, the cells could come from something unknown.

Each cell in a living thing has a copy of the same DNA, arranged in a double helix shape such as this.

Making sense of it all

Now you've seen the evidence, it's time to make up your own mind. The Mystery Master is looking for answers. Do you think you'll be able to provide them? What do you think are the most important pieces of evidence that will convince people that the Yeti exists? Maybe you agree with those people who say the Yeti is just a legend, or a brown bear.

Bears standing on their hind legs could be mistaken for giant apes from a distance.

INVESTIGATION TIPS

Yeti tourists

Is it possible that some of the evidence about Yetis and other cryptids has been deliberately faked? Can you think of reasons why people would do that? Stories of strange creatures such as Bigfoot, the Loch Ness Monster and the Yeti can often bring many visitors to the area where these creatures live. These visitors make money for hotels, restaurants and shops.

Who are the key witnesses?

There's no doubt that many people believe the Yeti exists. Some of them, such as the Sherpa people, have lived in the heart of the Himalayas for generations. Others are experienced and world-renowned mountaineers who believe they have seen or heard an animal they can't explain. Do you think there's enough evidence for you to decide that there is still something out there to be discovered?

What other evidence can you use?

Science can help us study the evidence, and sometimes confirm that Yeti relics and fur samples belong to other animals like the serow. Most scientists keep an open mind about the natural world, knowing that there are still undiscovered species out there.

Just because someone's seen a shaggy primate wandering through the woods, that doesn't make it a fact. These days, science can analyse the tiniest fragment of fur and find out where it came from. If the Yeti's out there somewhere, where's the scientific evidence to prove it?

Will we ever solve this mystery?

New advances in science, such as DNA testing, are helping to solve the mystery of the Yeti. We can now discover beyond doubt if a piece of fur or bone belonged to a known or unknown animal. But science can't prove that the Yeti is just a legend, only that we need more evidence to solve the mystery.

Today, more climbers visit the Himalayas than ever before. So far, these visitors have not found proof that the Yeti exists, and there are worries that their impact could damage the environment.

Some explorers who spent years investigating this mystery have made up their minds. Reinhold Messner even believed he had seen the Yeti himself. In the end, he decided it was probably a bear. Edmund Hillary found it impossible to separate the real Yeti from the legends surrounding it. Anthony Wooldridge was sure he'd seen a Yeti, and his photos seemed to be genuine. Only later did he discover his Yeti was a rock.

To prove that Yetis are roaming the Himalayas, the best evidence would be the capture of a live Yeti. In more than half a century of expeditions to find the Yeti, no one has come close to achieving this.

The problem with eyewitness reports, photos and even film is that, up to now, they leave too many questions unanswered. Unless the same thing is witnessed by many people, there will always be suspicions that it has been faked.

TOP SECRET

If the Yeti does exist, it could be under threat like many other animals. Earth's climate is getting warmer because of human industry and transport fumes. This could threaten the cold habitat where the Yeti supposedly roams. Time may be running out to solve this mystery.

What would happen if we did find the Yeti?

We all hope that the newly discovered Yeti would be protected and left in peace in its remote home. However, there is a risk that it would be targeted by hunters or disturbed by thousands of tourists bringing litter and pollution to the Himalayas.

If the Yetis are out there, maybe they are wise to keep out of sight.

TOP SECRET

In 2010, Chinese hunters believed they had captured a Yeti. It had four legs and no hair. Later it was revealed that the strange creature was a civet, a cat-like animal that does not share any similarities with typical descriptions of a Yeti.

Whether it is real or not, the Yeti will always be part of the legends of the mountains.

INVESTIGATION TIPS

Keep asking questions

You may think you've solved this mystery, but there's always more to find out. Keep asking questions and looking for new scientific discoveries about the Yeti. Look at the Find out more section at the end of this book to pursue new lines of enquiry.

WILD WORLD

There are stories of mystery primates all over the world. The Yeti and Bigfoot are the most famous, but some others have gained less global fame:

- Yowie: A "wild man" that is believed to roam the Australian wilderness.
- Orang-pendek: The name of this ape means "short man" and it is believed to live in the jungles of Sumatra, Asia.
- Yeren: Believed to live in the mountains and forests of China.
- Hibagon: This foul-smelling Japanese ape is said to be much smaller than the Yeti or Bigfoot.

TOP SECRET

The Mani Rimdu festival is celebrated in October or November in Nepal. At the end of the festival, the monks perform a masked dance and one of them will play the part of the Yeti.

TIMELINE

326 BCE
Alexander the Great demands to see a Yeti during his invasion of the Indus Valley civilization close to the Himalayas

1925
Photographer N.A. Tombazi records the sighting of an ape-like creature during an expedition to the Himalayas

1959
Peter Byrne takes one finger of a "Yeti's hand" from a monastery in Nepal. Later tests show that this finger is human.

1955
Hiker William Roe claims to have seen Bigfoot or Sasquatch while out walking

1900

1800 CE   **1925**   **1950**   **1960**

1921
An expedition exploring the route to Mount Everest discovers tracks in the snow. Stories of an "Abominable Snowman" appear in British newspapers.

1951
Climber Eric Shipton photographs "Yeti footprints" during an expedition to Mount Everest

1960
Edmund Hillary sets out on his own expedition to find the truth about the Yeti. The expedition reveals that a supposed yeti scalp is actually from another animal.

1832 CE
Brian Hodgson, a British adventurer visiting Nepal, reports sighting of a "wild man"

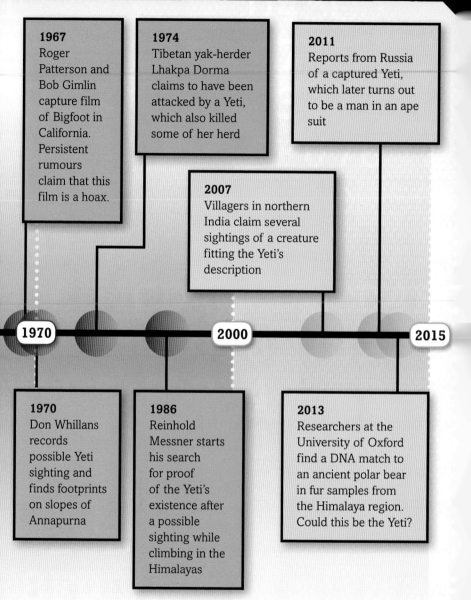

1967
Roger Patterson and Bob Gimlin capture film of Bigfoot in California. Persistent rumours claim that this film is a hoax.

1974
Tibetan yak-herder Lhakpa Dorma claims to have been attacked by a Yeti, which also killed some of her herd

2011
Reports from Russia of a captured Yeti, which later turns out to be a man in an ape suit

2007
Villagers in northern India claim several sightings of a creature fitting the Yeti's description

1970

2000

2015

1970
Don Whillans records possible Yeti sighting and finds footprints on slopes of Annapurna

1986
Reinhold Messner starts his search for proof of the Yeti's existence after a possible sighting while climbing in the Himalayas

2013
Researchers at the University of Oxford find a DNA match to an ancient polar bear in fur samples from the Himalaya region. Could this be the Yeti?

GLOSSARY

altitude height above sea level

ancestor person or animal from which another is descended

carnivore animal that eats meat

crevasse deep, open crack in a glacier or sheet of ice

cryptid animal or plant whose existence has been suggested but never proven by scientists

cryptozoology study of, and searches for, proof of cryptids. Someone who studies cryptozoology is called a cryptozoologist.

DNA (deoxyribonucleic acid) material in living cells that carries information about how a living thing looks and functions

enigma mystery or puzzle

eyewitness person who sees something happen, such as by being present at an event

forensic relating to scientific techniques to solve crimes or mysteries

frostbite damage to body parts such as fingers and toes caused by extreme cold

glacier slow-moving river of ice formed by snow and ice on high mountains

Global Positioning System (GPS) device that uses satellites to accurately plot someone's position

hoax trick or practical joke designed to fool people

ice axe tool used by mountaineers to help them climb icy slopes

legend traditional story that may be based in historical fact

livestock animals kept to provide food or other products

myth type of traditional story, which often involves supernatural ideas

Native American name for several peoples who lived in the Americas before their lands were discovered and colonized by Europeans

Neanderthal species of human that is believed to have become extinct around 35,000 years ago

permit official document to show that someone is allowed to do something

predator animal that eats or preys on other animals

primate mammal of the group that includes humans, apes, lemurs and monkeys

scalp skin and hair covering the top of the head

serow one of several species similar to a goat or antelope, and found in the Himalayas

Sherpa people living on the border of Nepal and Tibet, in the Himalayas

snow-line altitude above which mountains are always covered in snow because it is too cold for snow to melt

species type of animal. Members of the same species look similar and can breed together.

FIND OUT MORE

Are you still looking for answers? You can find more about yetis and possible sightings in your local library, or by searching online. Here are a few ideas about where to look next.

Books

Bigfoot and the Yeti, Mary Colson (Raintree, 2013)

Half-human Monsters and Other Fiends, Ruth Owen (Bearport, 2013)

Strange Animals, Rupert Matthews (QED, 2011)

Surviving in the Wilderness, Michael Hurley (Raintree, 2012)

Websites

There's more evidence out there to explore. When looking at websites, think about who has written the information and whether it includes the views and evidence of scientific experts. Follow these website links to keep on the trail of the Yeti:

channel.nationalgeographic.com/videos/evidence-of-the-yeti
A short video explores the story behind Shipton's famous photographs of Yeti footprints.

www.nhm.ac.uk/about-us/news/2014/july/proof-of-the-yeti-not-quite-yet131891.html
The Natural History Museum website includes information on the latest Yeti discoveries.

www.unmuseum.org/yeti.htm
This article is about the legend of the Yeti.

Exploring further

You'll be able to find lots of wild ideas online about the existence of the Yeti and other incredible creatures. You could look into the stories and evidence of other cryptids such as Bigfoot and the Loch Ness Monster.

Sources of information you can trust include museums such as the Natural History Museum in London, as well as journals and news sources such as the BBC or National Geographic.

Films

Mysterious monsters feature in many different films and television programmes, such as the giant ape *King Kong* or the dinosaurs of *Jurassic World*. These show our endless fascination with mysterious monsters. Look out for documentary films such as National Geographic's *Abominable Snowman*, which follows the trail of the Yeti in the dramatic scenery of the Himalayas.

INDEX